MOTOWN AND ME

A Tribute To The Music I Love

By

International Vocalist

Steve Simone

Dedication

I would like to thank God for always guiding me in good times and in bad, to my wife and son for helping me find my passion and giving me the strength to pursue it. To my sister and her husband, who believed in me when I found it hard to believe in myself, and my nieces, who are an inspiration. And to my brother and his family – I am so grateful that we finally had a chance to reconcile.

This book is a long time in the making. It spans many years as a vocalist and artist, and so many people have inspired my creativity.

To all of them, I give my thanks.

Table of Contents

Chapter 1

<u>My Story</u>

I was born in Islington, London and raised by my grandmother in Long Island, New York. I embraced music from an early age, and my first school concert was performed at the age of eight.

Ever since I was a young boy, I had always loved soul music and the artists that made it, from James Brown to The Drifters to labels such as Motown and Stax. I always knew I wanted to be a singer. I don't believe I had idols as such - more artists I admired for the way they sang and presented themselves on stage, with dynamic sounds and fantastic dance moves. I just knew that I would one day be like them, except for the dance moves, I have two left feet.

My journey started when I performed Johnny Mathis's *"When a Child Is Born"* at my school. I remember wearing out at least three singles when there were no downloads, and you had to choose between 45s and 78s. I was trying to capture the song's essence and noting every breath taken at every phrase that made this song so magical at the time. I was also interested in the theatre and joined the Anna Sher children's theatre, working with many of the kids that would appear on Grange Hill and EastEnders.

My formative years were spent in New York, where I was raised by my grandmother and my uncles. We lived on Long Island in a nice, safe part of the city. From what I recall, it was a happy time. However, I don't remember anything up to the age of 13 besides the occasional flashback. I certainly don't remember my time in Islington or my biological father, whom I have been searching for over 30 years, so at the time, New York life was all I knew.

At the age of five, I contracted meningitis, chickenpox and measles and was pronounced dead three times. I survived by the grace of God and am still here to tell my story.

When I returned to the UK to live with my mother and stepfather, I was drawn to the theatre and amateur dramatics. My first play at school was called "The Children's Crusade" and then Shakespeare's "*A Mid-Summer Night's Dream*". I've always liked the old English language and studied it a great deal while at school. When I was 18, I got the chance to perform in Sir Gawain and the Green Knight at the Minack Theatre in Cornwall.

As a young man, I undertook many different roles in the workplace, from toilet cleaner to working at Harrods department store in Knightsbridge. My first full time job was working at Thames television on a YTS or (youth training scheme) I was privileged to work with some the most memorable stars of television at the time like Benny Hill, Leonard Rositter Of Rising damp, Bucks Fizz fresh of their Eurovision win and Eamon Andrew's of "This Is Your Life" to name a few, One thing that comes to mind while working at Thames, when I was at the Euston Studios and was asked to put a microphone on the Duke Of Edinburgh who had come to promote his book on a show called "Mavis" and the sound guys almost scared me to death telling me the consequences of doing it wrong, on the day I was very nervous but Prince Philip put my mind at ease. I also at this time found my passion for photography and was a press photographer for ten years. I covered concerts and had the great honor of taking shots of some of the greatest artists on the planet, Michael Jackson, Janet Jackson, Gloria Estefan and MC Hammer, to name a few. My first assignment was at the Marque Club in London, where I covered Dave Stewart of the Eurythmics and then Candy Dulfer, what made it even more memorable was the fact I could talk my way backstage and was able to meet them. I also covered Steve Davis's wedding, the FA Cup and Crufts. I also worked as an official photographer for Bernardo's and covered many events that including the Queen Mother's 90th Birthday in 1990. I really enjoyed my time as a press photographer but left the profession when it started getting more cutthroat. Throughout my various jobs, the influence of music never left me, and I found myself rehearsing new songs every time I heard a tune that moved me. I eventually went back to music by joining Butlins.

I joined the London Hotel in Bayswater, where I worked as a Redcoat, trying to soak in as much as possible. I remember watching Lee Pashley performing on my second day and his amazing voice captured me with a song called "Boy from Nowhere" by Tom Jones. This song was amazing, telling the story of a matador called El Cordobes.

While at Butlins, I worked with differing styles of music and artists who came to perform each week, it was a great experience, but I was ready to move on after a year, so I went to Pontins as a Bluecoat, the first black Bluecoat entertainer in the UK. Pontins was not a great time for me, but I gained the knowledge I needed to move on.

As with all professions, you must start at the bottom and work your way up; at least, that is what I had always believed. As a singer, I started working in pubs and clubs, getting a name for myself as a solo artist, and working with tribute groups in honor of bands such as The Drifters, The Four Tops and The Temptations. I worked with many different artists and had the pleasure of working with some hugely recognizable names. I attended many showcases and got work around the country, but as much as I enjoyed it, I wanted more, including traveling worldwide.

So that's exactly what I set out to do.

MARRIED LIFE

I met my wife while working in Spain as an entertainer. After finishing my contract, I visited her in Northern Ireland and moved there from Bath. I had been to Northern Ireland ten years before I met her - mainly because people told me not to go. I was always skeptical about what I read in newspapers and wanted to experience it myself. I found it so amazingly friendly and welcoming when I first arrived. As I travelled around, I was always greeted by lovely people who weren't concerned about where I was from or what religion I belonged to - it was truly a wonderful experience. I started working on the cabaret circuit in Ireland and worked with many of the major players in the country music scene, but I found it to be a lot of work for little reward. So, I set my sights on cruise ships.

CRUISING

I started working on cruises about 20 years ago, my first ship was the Aussonia run by Louis Cruise Lines where I worked as an entertainer. And then started singing on Airtours cruises then Island Star and Island Escape. During a conversation with a passenger, I was asked if I ever considered lecturing as my show was like a history lesson. I had never considered talking about music rather than singing it, but I thought about it and decided to try it out, not knowing whether it would work. I firmly believe in *"if you never try, you'll never know,"* so I took the plunge. My first cruise as a speaker was on the P&O Aurora, leaving from Tahiti to Southampton with Roy Walker and a few other celebrities. I arrived at Heathrow the night before and left my bags in the left luggage at the airport. Hearing music coming from the upper floor, I went to investigate. Staff were collecting money for Comic Relief and had put on a karaoke, so I sang a song, donated, and went on my way. The next day, we were getting ready to board our flight to LAX, and the attendant collected my ticket and ripped it up. As you can imagine, I was a little confused. He told me that they enjoyed my rendition of Stand by Me the night before so much that they had upgraded me!

Performing remains my absolute passion - when I hear albums such as Stevie Wonder's *"Songs in the Key of Life,"* it feels like replaying the soundtrack to my life. I remain so inspired by the artists I hear, and the imagery in their songs still speaks to me. The Four Tops, Temptations, Marvin Gaye, and so many others were sounds I used to get me through the hard times (what I thought were hard, but looking back, they really weren't). Being able to perform them for a living makes me feel extremely fortunate, and I'm so glad I stuck with my dream of pursuing entertainment as a career. Knowing how much the music resonates with my audiences makes it even more of a privilege.

VILAMOURA

On the way to achieving my goal of performing on cruises, I did a lot of gigs both around Ireland and the UK, which often mention a lot of travel from one venue to another, I have to give my wife a special mention as if was not for her I wouldn't have been able to do the work that I've done, sometime sleeping in the car to the next day and travelling hours on to different venues, changing in fast food restaurants and eating at two in the morning on the way home, this is familiar to all of us that have gigged or are still gigging.

Then I went to Portugal, with a group called Wheels of Motown were put together to appeal to an international audience working with "Belinda King Presents" an hour and half round the world dance show. I met Max and Floyd two great singers in Wales, and we rehearsed our show a fifteen-minute set in the middle of the dance show. So after rehearsing the set we flew to Vilamoura, Portugal were we met Alan Cutler and Belinda King and her dancers, and on opening night as you can imaging everyone was full of nerves and excitement, we were waiting in the wings to go on, and thought it very quiet, so we went out do our fives songs along with the choreographs steps and there was no reaction by the audience so were looking at each other thinking, what did we do wrong, we left the stage and nothing, we notice that there wasn't really any reaction to any of the dances either, so were all thinking they might not have liked the show, so the last dance ends the entire crowd erupts into rapturous applause, standing ovation as dancers were presented and then we came on stage to take our bows the crowd got louder as we left the stage, we felt amazing. When we got back, I did a few gigs with Max a Floyd and as always happens we went our separate ways. I hope that whatever they are doing now they are both well.

Ibiza

I was contacted to join a group in Ibiza, when I arrived I was part of a three piece group performing Soul and Motown. They were not the easiest of people to work with and I found myself doing most of the songs in the show while they danced and took two songs each in a hour and half show. This went on for a while until the day that I simply had enough and left, expecting harsh word from my employers I got ready the worst, but surprisingly I received a email informing me that the two other members had a been let go and asking my if I would come back with my own show. I preformed my shows in Ibiza for five years and absolutely loved it.

LECTURES

The more I researched artists and labels, the more interested and fascinated I became with the music, not only Soul/Motown but also Jazz and Reggae. The lives behind the music had me equally gripped: artists like Bob Marley, Stevie Wonder, Marvin Gaye, Sam Cooke, and so many more. While researching Lionel Richie, I stumbled across the Tuskegee Airmen, who were the first all-black air squadron in the US Air Force, known as the Red Tails. This then piqued my interest in African American history, so I started a series dealing with this subject that included Frederick Douglas, Harriet Tubman, and The Underground Railroad, and much more.

My ambition is to start working on many other projects, both in music and in lecturing, working on new songs and recording.

Chapter 2

<u>Motown</u>

In addition to sharing my own story, my vision and motivation for writing this book is to tell the story of Motown and pay tribute to the music, artists, and producers I love. So, let's go back to where it all started.

BERRY GORDY JR.

In 1958, Berry Gordy Jr. and William "Smokey" Robinson set about creating a place for artists to live their dreams in Detroit. Berry Gordy Jnr had always loved music and wanted to be a singer but found his talent wasn't good enough then, so he decided to write songs. "Higher & Higher" and "Lonely Teardrops" were both penned by Berry and were major hits for one of the biggest artists at the time, Jackie Wilson.

After a stint in the army, where he served in the Korean War and was a semi-professional boxer and was on the same bill as the famous Joe Lewis, Berry returned to his family home in Detroit. His father - affectionately named "Pops" - had one rule in his house: if you lived under his roof, you had to work, so Berry, still wanting to be a part of the music industry, decided to open a jazz record store. Unfortunately, it didn't do well and closed, so he returned to his passion for making music. His sister Anna owned a small record label, and Berry convinced his family co-op to loan him $800, which he used to cut his first single with artist Barrett Strong. *Money (That's What I Want)* was penned by Gordy and later became a hit for the Beatles.

Together with a long-time friend and singer, William "Smokey" Robinson, they bought a house at 2648 West Grand Boulevard on January 12, 1958. This would become the headquarters for the newly formed Tamla Motown Record label.

Berry Gordy's vision for Motown was revolutionary for its time, and he ensured that all his artists were the best they could be before meeting the world. We should all be grateful for his contribution to music.

THE EARLY YEARS

Motown was founded by two friends with a dream to make music, and they accomplished that dream relatively fast, considering the political landscape in America at the time. The civil rights movement had just started gaining traction on the home and world stage, and Martin Luther King Jr and Malcolm X were prominent leaders. Although they had the same goal, they had distinctly differing viewpoints: one advocated for peaceful protest and the other violent retaliation. Amid the chaos, two labels were born - on the East Coast Motown and the West Coast Stax. Both invited artists to perform, with no color bar to hold them back from making inspirational music.

The label was founded initially as Tamla Motown Records due to a successful film called Tammy that starred Debbie Reynolds. Tamla was eventually dropped for Motown, which stood for Motor-Town, the home of the Ford production plant, in Detroit where the label was based.

The most crucial element of any record label is its artists; Motown was no exception. All were amazingly talented, but unlike today, where your fate is decided by how good you are on a TV show or social media, Motown artists were chosen based on pure talent. This was a complicated and intense process; Berry Gordy was a strict taskmaster and required all his acts to be the best they could be (at least in front of an audience). Once you were accepted on the label, you had many hoops that you would have to go through to get to the finished product. Many artists went through the process, but few made the final cut.

The earliest group to make it onto the Motown roster was Smokey Robinson and the Miracles, formed by Smokey, a Detroit native and co-founder of the Tamla Motown Label. This was the first group to put Motown on the map.

"Shop Around" by Smokey Robinson and the Miracles was the first big hit for the young label and brought together classy suits and choreographed dance moves that had never been seen before. In addition to the music, Berry thought about his acts and how they behaved professionally, so he employed voice coaches and etiquette coaches to make sure the whole label had a polished and professional look.

Motown was made up of artists, musicians, writers, and producers who were the best in their field and represented the beating heart of Detroit talent. They were discovered while working in bars and clubs. For example, The Funk Brothers were the house band at Motown and were picked mainly by Mickey Stevenson, a producer at the label who toured the bars and clubs hand-picking musicians. Earl Van Dyke, the charismatic and fun-loving band leader, and James Jamerson, an extraordinary bass player, made the Motown sound so distinctive.

Chapter 3

The Civil Rights Movement

Music was an instrument for change and helped defeat the racial segregation in the United States in the 60s. Everyone played a part in tearing down the wall that divided a nation, from Sammy Davis Jnr to Motown and Stax Records.

There were many heroes who wanted to change the racist climate that existed in the United States in the 60s, but nothing made more of an impact than music. Let's go back to June 19th 1865 (known as Juneteenth), when the enslaved people were set free from savage conditions and harsh treatment they'd endured at the hands of enslavers, and in the civil rights movement of the 1950s and 1960s, music always had its place in the long history of the struggle for freedom and equality. From Harriet Tubman's *"Wade in the Water,"* a signal for slaves to stay hidden in the water so as not to get the attention of slave catchers, to Sam Cooke's *"A Change Gone Come,"* inspired by Bob Dylan's *"Blowing in the Wind."*

SAMMY DAVIS JNR

Sammy Davis Jnr was born in in Harlem, New York in 1925. He started performing at the age of three with his father and uncle in a Vaudeville show. As he grew, he became friends with Frank Sinatra, and Dean Martin and Peter Lawford were known collectively as "The Rat Pack", however they were not the first "Rat Pack" that distinction would go to Lauren Bacall, Humphrey Bogart and James Cagney.

He lost his eye in 1954 in a road traffic accident. He joined Motown in 1970 and recorded "Live Carnegie Hall", and a controversial Album "Something for Everyone". Even though he was a very successful and sort after artist, he was subjected to racism and discrimination because he involved with Kim Novak in 1957, she was under contract with Columbia pictures, Harry Cohn president of Columbia gave into pressure to threaten Davis as this relationship was hurting the studio's reputation. He was also not invited to the JFK's inauguration due to him marrying a Swedish actress, Mary Britt.

MARTIN LUTHER KING JNR

Martin Luther King Jnr was the greatest civil rights leader in America. He refused to bow down to white supremacy and led a movement to change the hearts and souls of a nation by nonviolent means. He was subsidized by Harry Belafonte, who was able to help the family because, as a preacher, he only earned $800 a month. Belafonte was also responsible for organizing *Freedom Summer,* which unfortunately was also known as *"Mississippi Burning,"* where three civil rights activists were found dead in a levy. This event also appears in Don McClean's *"American Pie."*

MOTOWN CIVIL RIGHTS SONGS

When Marvin Gaye released *"What's Going On"* in May 1971, it totally changed Motown and the message that it was sending. Before this, Motown was mainly a fun label singing about love and good times; now, they were dealing with social issues, and change was coming. When Stevie Wonder released "Songs in The Key Of Life" in September 1976, it sealed the deal - Motown was dealing with a new generation looking for change, and they were paving the way for this to happen. Artists refused to play shows in the South until organizers took down the rope that divided their black and white audiences. This and many other events played their part in breaking down the barriers that divided the nation for so long.

These were just some of the civil rights songs Motown produced:

- What's Going On - Marvin Gaye
- Ball of Confusion - The Temptations
- Flower Child - David Ruffin
- War - Edwin Star
- Living for the City - Stevie Wonder
- Abraham, Martin & John - Marvin Gaye (written by the Bee Gees)

It seemed that the climate was changing for everyone. Almost all record labels, from Motown to Stax were producing protest songs. And unfortunately, those songs are as relevant today as they were when they were released.

CHAPTER 4

The Artists I Love

There are so many amazing artists associated with the Motown label, more than 230 at my last count, which means this book would take significantly longer to write if I featured them all! So, in this section, I have selected the artists who had the most significant impact on me personally and whose influences are most reflected in my performances.

THE COMMODORES

Lionel Richie was born in Tuskegee, Alabama, and he formed a group on his college campus at Tuskegee University. This prestigious place was the home of the Tuskegee Airmen, the first African American Pilots in the United States Airforce. He was born in 1949, and while at college, he formed the Commodores, signed to Atlantic Records in 1968, then moved to Motown and supported the Jackson 5 in Harlem. They had a string of successful songs, including *"Machine Gun," "Brick," "Easy,"* and *"Three time a Lady"*. The group split up when Motown moved to California, and Lionel pursued his solo career. After the split, the Commodores had one hit, *"Nightshift,"* without Lionel as lead singer.

DIANA ROSS AND THE SUPREMES

Originally called the Primettes, the Supremes were set up as a vocal R&B group. Its members were all brought up in the Brewster Projects in Detroit. Coming from modest means, they thrived in their environment, and music was the perfect outlet to improve their lives and hone their talent.

Florence Ballard, who was the lead singer in the Primettes at the time, had a fantastic silky voice and seemed to be able to sing anything put in front of her. But Diana Ross's striking vocals better suited the image Motown was looking for. She became lead singer when the group moved to Motown and was renamed the Supremes. Later, to become Diana Ross and the Supremes became the undisputed First Ladies of Motown with a string of hits that could not be rivalled.

The Four Tops

This legendary group that all met while attending college was a fine example of dedication to the music they made and each other. Levi Stubbs, Lawrence Patton, Obie Ben-son and Abdul Fakir were all amazing singers in their own right, but when they came together, magic was made.

They were formerly known as The Aims, but to ensure there was no confusion with The Aims Brothers, their name was changed to the Four Tops when they came to Motown. Together, they had a string of hits that spanned over 30 years.

Marvin Gaye

Marvin Pentz Gay Jr. was born in Washington, DC, in 1939 to a lay preacher and homemaker. His father was the pastor of the Church of God ministry, a very strict sect of Christianity. Marvin grew up in a very confused family owing to its strict religious beliefs. While holding a position within the church and the community, his father was also a cross-dresser. This was widely known in the family's neighborhood, which made Marvin a target for bullying. Marvin was a very tall, handsome man who found no problems flirting with the opposite sex, but he was always conflicted and never found true connections.

MARVIN MEETS ANNA GORDY

Anna Gordy was born on January 28, 1922, and was Berry's older sister. She was a businesswoman, songwriter, and producer. She met Marvin when he performed with the New Moonglows, led by Harvey Fuqua, in 1959. They started dating in 1960, by which time Anna Records had been absorbed into Motown, and were married in June 1963.

By all accounts, their relationship was turbulent, and to calm the tension, they adopted a boy, Marvin Pentz Gay III, who was born in November 1966. His biological mother was Anna's niece, Denise Gordy. They moved to Hollywood in 1971 and filed for a trial separation two years later. In 1975, Gordy filed for divorce, and two years later, a settlement was agreed upon, which included an agreement that Marvin would remit a portion of his royalties from his album. The album was called "*Here My Dear*" and cataloged the ups and downs of the marriage. Anna later reconciled with Marvin and would accompany him to many industry events. She died on January 31, 2014, at the age of 92.

Although Marvin's personal life was challenging, his music career faired a little better. His commanding officer in the Army noted that Marvin "did not like to follow orders." This would lead to some conflicts in his civilian life. After being discharged from the army, he joined The Moonglows, a doo-wop group headed by Harvey Fuqua. Fuqua met Marvin while performing with The Marquees after working for a while with The Moonglows. Motown drafted him as a producer, taking Marvin with him.

When he joined the label, Marvin's main role was as a drummer, and he became part of the Funk Brothers for a short while. Motown then realized what talent they had in Marvin, and he became a prominent artist on the label. Marvin always thought himself a crooner in the shape of his idol Sam Cooke (the reason he added an 'e' to his name), but Motown had other ideas, and conflict often arose when he was made to stretch his range. His objection to authority was evident when he wrote "*What's Going On*," a thought-provoking sensitive album inspired by his brother's letter to him from the front line in Vietnam. This was a radical change in direction for the label, which up to that time had mainly produced what was known in the industry as 'bubblegum' pop that appealed to the masses. He and Berry Gordy nearly came to blows over the album, but ever the businessman, Berry conceded to his artist's request and released the album to instant acclaim. This gave Marvin the success he craved after constantly feeling like he never fully reached his potential. But as the saying goes, 'be careful what you wish for' - with success came other demons such as drug abuse, toxic relationships and many financial problems, not least owing the IRS $5000.000 in back taxes. All this led to him living in a camper van on a beach, where, fortunately for him, a boxing promoter took him under his wing, flew him to Belgium and got him clean.

Now, back to his old self, Marvin started making music once more, and while in Belgium, he released Sexual Healing, which became a worldwide hit. Unfortunately, true to form, his demons once again followed his success, and he reverted to his old habits. After moving back to the family home, one fateful day, an argument escalated to the point that his father shot him with a gun Marvin had bought him (he was later to die in prison for his crime).

MARY WELLS

Mary Ester Wells was born on May 13, 1943, in Detroit. She was a very sickly child and had spinal meningitis at a young age, which caused her to be partially blind and deaf in one ear. Mary also contracted tuberculosis at the age of 10. Music was her means of escape, and she sang in church choirs and progressed to nightclubs.

When she was 17, she approached Berry Gordy with a song she had written for Jackie Wilson called *"Bye Bye Baby,"* but he insisted she sing it to him. Impressed with her performance, he signed her to his label in September 1960. She became the first Mo-town female artist to have a top 40 pop single after Mickey Steven penned *"I Don't Want to Take a Chance."* It hit 33 on the Billboard chart in June 1961. In 1964, she released her most famous single, *"My Guy,"* which became her trademark single written by Smokey Robinson. It crossed over to the Billboard Hot 100 and knocked Lions Armstrong's *Hello Dolly* from number 1, remaining there for two weeks and becoming her second million-selling single.

MICHAEL JACKSON

Michael was born on August 29, 1958, in a small town in Indiana called Gary. He lived in a modest house with his parents, Joe and Katherine and his siblings Randy, Tito, Jermaine, Marlon, Janet and Latoya. Joe was a steelworker and frustrated musician, and his mother, Kathrine, was a homemaker and devoted Jehovah's Witness. Joe was a very strict influence, and Katherine had more of a calming personality. From a young age, their children showed great musical talent and often performed the hits of the day for their mother. Joe's main rule was that no one was allowed to touch his guitar, which his kids often broke while at work. One day, when Joe returned home early, he found his guitar being played by Tito as the Jackson children performed for their mother. Fearful of what came next, to their great surprise, Joe did not get upset or send them out for a switch (a type of tree often used as a form of punishment); he sat down and asked them to play. After the initial shock, Tito nervously played, and Jermaine sang. Impressed, Joe contacted a friend who had contacts in the music industry.

The siblings were initially signed to Steels town Records, but after a talent show at the High Chaparral nightclub, they met Bobby Taylor, who signed them up for Motown. Berry was reluctant to take on child artists as he knew the complexities it entailed, but after seeing an audition tape, he was convinced to sign them to the label. The Jackson 5 were pushed to succeed by their producer Ronnie Taylor, and their first hit was in Oct '69 with "*I Want You Back*," a song that defined what would be known as bubblegum soul.

The Jackson 5 had massive success in the US and the UK with a string of unmatched hits at the time. In 1971 on the set of The Wiz (the African American remake of The Wizard of Oz), Michael met the man that would shape his future and make him the supreme King Of Pop. His name was Quincy Jones.

Quincy was an award-winning music producer and musician. He noticed Michael when they were conversing about Socrates - when Michael mispronounced it, Quincy put him straight.

By this point, as a solo artist, Michael decided to sign up to leave Motown and move to Quest Records, Quincy's record label. Their first offering was the album *Off the Wall,* which became a platinum-selling album and shot up the Billboard chart.

Michael first met Quincy Jones at Sammy Davis Jr's House at the age of twelve, they were watching the Ed Sullivan Show that featured the Jacksons, and their paths would not cross again until they met on the set of "The Wiz," where he played the scarecrow. He had released "Ben" and approached Quincy to ask if he would produce his next record. Despite pushback from record executives, they went ahead and produced his first solo album, *"Off the Wall,"* *"Thriller*, "and *"Bad."*

STEVIE WONDER

Stevie Wonder was born Stevland Hardaway Judkins on May 30, 1950, in Saginaw, Michigan and was also known as Stevland Hardaway Morris. His mother, Lula May Hardaway, had three boys – Larry, Milton, and Stevie, the middle child. He was born six weeks premature, and a condition called Retinopathy of prematurity caused him to go blind. His father, Calvin Judkins, was the third of six children. At age four, his parents divorced, and his mother moved him and his siblings to Detroit. Shortly after moving, Lula Mae changed his surname to Morris, which remains his legal surname.

After being discovered by Ronnie White of The Miracles, he and his mother were taken to see Berry Gordy, who signed him to the label. He then signed songwriter and producer Clarence Paul, who mentored and nicknamed him Little Stevie Wonder. He was signed to the label at the age of 11 and could play harmonica, piano, and drums by then. Because of his young age, his royalties were held in trust until he reached 21. He was given a tutor while he was on tour and paid $2.50 a week ($20.50).

Stevie was a curious child and took every opportunity to learn new instruments by working with The Funk Brothers. He wanted to know all he could about music, from singing to writing and producing, and he quickly became proficient in all aspects. From prank calls to all sorts of mischief, Stevie kept everyone on their toes as they wondered what else he would get up to.

Stevie's contract was re-negotiated when he reached the age of twenty-one and had just recorded his legendary album "*Songs In The Key Of Life*." Berry Gordy agreed to a 13-million-dollar renewal as well as all artist rights to the music he wrote, produced and played on.

Stevie also played an active role in the civil rights movement and was arrested several times for protesting about the rights of black people in America. His biggest triumph came when he got Martin Luther King Jnr's birthday on January 15, 1929, recognized as an official holiday, signed by Ronald Reagan on November 2, 1983, against much opposition. To celebrate this occasion, Stevie Wonder wrote "*Happy Birthday*."

As we now know, Stevie has become one of the most visionary artists of the 20th century.

THE MIRACLES

Later known as Smokey Robinson and the Miracles, this band was crucially important to the success of the Motown label. They were the first group from the Tamla Motown label to have great success with "*Shop Around*." They also featured female vocalist Claudette Roger Robinson, who stopped performing with the group in 1964 and is married to lead singer Smokey.

THE TEMPTATIONS

Also known as The Temptin' Temptations, these guys were the brainchild of Otis Williams, formerly of the Primes. All had a keen ear for music and were hungry to make their mark on the world.

The members were Eddie Kendricks, Paul Williams, Otis Williams, Melvin Franklin and singer Elbridge "AL" Bryant, who was replaced by David Ruffin as singer after his untimely death from liver cirrhosis when they joined Motown.

A chance meeting brought them to Berry Gordy's attention, and they auditioned for Mo-town. Berry reportedly liked the audition but wanted them to change their name at the time: Otis Williams and the Distance. They decided to call themselves "The Temptations". Like most of their fellow artists, it took them a while before they got a hit on the label, at one point being referred to as the "No Hit Temptations."

The group's fortunes started to change after David Ruffin was brought in place of Elbridge Bryant. Their 1965 hit "*My Girl*" was then firmly on the map, and the song, penned by Smokey Robinson, was to be Motown's first crossover hit. With success came a number of disagreements that were largely driven by Ruffin's well-documented ego, and he was eventually replaced by Eddie Kendrick, then Dennis Edwards.

THE VANDELLAS

The Vandellas was originally formed by Annette Beard, Rosalind Ashford and Gloria Williams and eventually included lead singer Martha Reeves after Williams left in 1962. Born July 18, 1941, in Alabama, Martha initially worked as a secretary at Motown. It's rumored that she overheard a conversation between Mickey Stephenson and Norman Whitfield, who was looking for a group to record, as the booked ones never showed up. Seeing an opportunity, Martha decided to put her group forward, and the rest, as they say, is history.

There are many other artists that I haven't mentioned in this book. Motown, as both a label and a music genre, has given us so many amazing artists that it's hard to count.

Chapter 5

Motown At The Movies

When Motown moved to Los Angeles in 1972, Berry Gordy had the idea of producing films. He accomplished his goal by making at least eleven, the most famous being *"Lady Sings the Blues,"* the tragic story of the life of Billie Holiday with Diana Ross as the lead alongside Billy Dee Williams. They also produced "The Wiz," which was a black adaptation of the "Wizard of Oz" – again, Diana Ross played the lead role of Dorothy, and Michael Jackson played the straw man. They also started the careers of leading black artists such as Richard Pryor and James Earl Jones.

Films Include:

- Almost Summer 1978
- The Bingo Long Traveling All-Stars & Motor Kings 1976 (sports comedy)
- The Jacksons: An American Dream 1992 (Miniseries)
- Lady Sings the Blues 1972
- The Last Dragon 1985 (Martial Arts Comedy)
- Mahogany 1975
- Scott Joplin 1979
- The Smokey Robinson Show 1970
- The Temptations 1998 (Miniseries)
- Thank God it's Friday 1978
- The Wiz 1978

All of the above films were produced by Berry Gordy, Motown Productions, and De Passé Jones Entertainment, which Suzanne De

Passé owned. She is a music, film and television producer and businesswoman who worked at Motown as a creative assistant to Berry Gordy.

25

Chapter 6

Motown: Behind The Music

Every company needs those behind the scenes that keep their operation running, just like a ship needs engineers, plumbers, electricians to keep the vessel afloat. You may not see them, but you know they are there because the ship is still moving, the lights are still on, and the water is still running. This is the story of the people who worked behind the scenes and were the backbone of Motown, the unsung heroes that you don't see and some who names you won't know. Without them, Motown would have never been internationally renowned la-bel.

When Motown was first set up Berry Gordy spent some time working at the Ford production plant in Detroit and paid close attention to how the production line ran from the start to finished product. He knew that if he wanted his venture to succeed he would have to run it like a production line. It wasn't good enough to be "ok" – the finished product had to be polished and perfect.

The label was made possible because of a loan given to Berry by his family, namely his sister Ester Gordy. Originally, he had asked for $1000 dollars, but Ester gave him $800, which Berry took and recorded a single that he wrote with Barrett Strong "Money (That's What I Want)" in 1959 which, as I mentioned in Chapter two, became a hit for the Beatles in 1963.

THE FIRST A&R MAN

The first person brought on to the label was William "Mickey" Stevenson who was the A&R director. When they first met, Mickey had come to Motown - as many did - wanting to be a singer. Berry listened to him and after he'd sung, asked "What else can you do"? Mickey said he had more songs but Berry told him he was looking for an A&R director and asked if he could do that instead. The rest was history.

Mickey's first job was to get musicians for Motown, and his first step was to assemble a band from local Detroit talent and call them The Funk Brothers". They hated the name but it stuck. Once he'd secured the session musicians, he went out looking for talent and was responsible for signing Stevie Wonder, The Temptations, The Four Tops and so many more. He was also responsible for bringing industry-leading writers and producers to Motown.

ASHFORD & SIMPSON

Nickolas Ashford born in South Carolina on May 4, 1941 and Valerie Simpson was born in the Bronx, New York, on August 26, 1946. Ashford & Simpson were amazing songwriters that both met in White Rock Baptist Church in 1964 and joined Motown in 1966. They started their careers in the mid-60s writing for Aretha Franklin and Ray Charles, and it was their work with Charles that brought them to Motown where they paired with Marvin Gaye and Tammi Terrell. They are responsible for such hits as *"Ain't No Mountain High Enough"*, *"Ain't Nothing Like the Real Thing"*, *"You're All I Need To Get By"* and also had success as a duo with their own release "Solid" in 1984.

BRIAN AND EDDIE HOLLAND

Edward James Holland Jnr was born in Detroit on the October 30 1939 and Brian Holland was born in Detroit February 15 1941.

The brothers worked with acts such as Martha and the Vandellas, The Supremes, The Four Tops and The Isley Brothers and were responsible for a lot of Motown's hits, as well as its legendary sound.

CHOLLY ATKINS

Born Charles Sylvan Atkinson in 1913 in Alabama, Cholly started dancing in the late 1930s before entering military service in WW2. He first found fame as a vaudeville act called "Atkins & Cole" who debuted at the Apollo theatre in Harlem. They performed extensively with many acts, from Louis Armstrong to Count Basie. In the mid-1950s Cholly began teaching dance steps to the Cadillacs, Shirelles, Moonglows, Franky Lymon, The Teenagers and many others. His style of teaching was coined as "Vocal Choreography" as vocalists enhanced their performances with stylish combinations and gestures. After working freelance for the Miracles in 1962, Atkins was hired to be Motown's choreographer in 1964.

CLARENCE PAUL

Clarence Otto Paul was born in North Carolina on the March 19 1928 and was a well-respected artist in his own right. He joined Motown as an artist development director and was responsible for the welfare of the children on the label. He started working with Stevie Won-der in 1960. He wrote, sang and produced, working with Gladys Knight, Stevie Wonder, The Jackson 5 and more.

THE FUNK BROTHERS

The Funk Brothers were the house band for Motown and were all hand-picked by Mickey Stevenson, mentioned earlier in this chapter. All had amazing skills and were a very closely guarded secret as Motown didn't want them to be poached by other labels.

LAMONT DOZIER

Lamont Herbert Dozier was born in Detroit on the June 16 1941. He was a singer, songwriter and producer who co-wrote and produced 14 US Billboard number one hits and four UK number ones. He joined Motown in 1962 and together with Brian and Eddie Holland, produced some of its most memorable songs.

MAXINE POWELL

Maxine was born on the May 15 1915 in Chicago. She was an etiquette instructor and talent agent and broke down many barriers as a black businesswoman and forward thinker. She made a name for herself as a model and then pursued an acting career before moving to Detroit in 1945 and opening her own finishing school in 1951. She closed her school in 1964 and became a consultant and talent agent for Motown, staying until 1969.

She initially met the Gordy family when she was looking for a printer to produce a poster for her annual fashion show and they were recommended to her. Some of the Gordy family at-tended her classes and she was approached by Berry Gordy to teach etiquette to his stable of artists.

She dealt with everyone from Smokey Robinson, Marvin Gaye and The Supremes to The Vandellas, and many more. In her own words "she came to teach them how to act."

NORMAN WHITFIELD

Norman Jessie Whitfield was born May 12, 1940 in Harlem. In his late teens he and his family moved to Detroit. When he was 19 he hung around the Motown offices. Recognized for his persistence, he got hired to work in the quality control department where decisions were made as to which singles would be released. He then joined the songwriting team, eventually taking over Smokey Robinson's role as lead writer for The Temptations. From 1966 to 1974 he produced all of The Temptations music.

RON MILLER

Ronald Norman Miller was born in Chicago on October 5, 1922 and was discovered by Berry Gordy and Mickey Stevenson in 1960. He was a songwriter and producer and wrote the smash hit "For Once in My Life" the night his daughter Angel was born. This was first record-ed by Barbara McNair and then went on to be a massive hit for Stevie Wonder.

Chapter 7

<u>Motown today</u>

Motown was sold to MCA Records in 1988 and many of their artists walked away from the label. Even though they were still producing songs after their move to LA, a lot of people believe that the magic they made in Detroit was never the same after the move. Berry Gordy still has a record label called Gordy Records and still signs artists – he has also produced "The Motown Musical" which has premiered on Broadway and the West End.

At the age of 94 he is still going strong alongside Smokey Robinson. They made their dreams a reality, as well as those of all those kids that sang on corners in Detroit.

Motown will always have an everlasting legacy that will never die.

TODAY'S MUSIC

As with many things in this world, music has moved on, and some say it has evolved into what we have today. In my opinion, the soul & R&B we used to know back in the 50s, 60s and 70s, when songs had meaning, a great melody and a sound, is nothing like the music of the same genre today.

When you hear the opening notes of James Jameson on his bass guitar playing "My Girl" you instantly know what it is - unfortunately the creativity has gone and they are sampling and rehashing old tunes and trying to put a modern twist to them, which in my opinion just doesn't work the majority of the time.

The one thing I've realized through the years is that music is generational - our kids listen to our music until they find a style they prefer and we did the same thing with our parents and their parents. Undoubtedly our parents hated our music as we hate our kids' music! You know you're getting old when you come out with the phrase "In my day" - I hate that phrase so much but find myself saying it more and more.

The one thing that spans all generations is the fact that music makes us feel something. It's not something that can be defined or measured – it's that inexplicable flicker of recognition we feel in our soul. That's what Motown is for me, and while the future will take care of itself, I'm happy to keep singing and paying tribute to the music I love.